SUMMER OF THE ALL-ROUNDER

For Kate

PATRICK EAGAR's photographs of cricket and cricketers have deservedly established him as the leading photographer of the game. In *A Summer to Remember* he brought brilliantly to life the thrilling Tests of 1981. In this book he has produced a no less memorable record of a season notable for the outstanding performances of three great all-rounders: Ian Botham, Kapil Dev, Imran Khan. The drama of all six Tests is here, and much else, captured in images and words.

ALAN ROSS's cricket books include *Australia 55, Cape Summer, Through the Caribbean* and *West Indies at Lord's*. He edited *The Cricketer's Companion*. From 1953–1972 he was cricket correspondent of the *Observer* and now writes for *The Times*. He played cricket and squash racquets for Oxford and the Royal Navy.

Test and Championship Cricket
in England 1982

SUMMER OF THE ALL-ROUNDER

PATRICK EAGAR

with commentary by Alan Ross

COLLINS
St James's Place, London, 1982

First Published in 1982
by William Collins Sons & Co Ltd
London · Glasgow · Sydney · Auckland
Toronto · Johannesburg

The pictures on pp 124–5 appear by
kind permission of the M.C.C.

Designed by Ronald Clark
Photoset in Century Schoolbook by
MS Filmsetting Ltd, Frome, Somerset and
Reproduction by Gilchrist Bros Ltd, London & Leeds
Printed and bound by Robert Hartnoll Ltd, Cornwall

ISBN 0 00 216631 3

CONTENTS

INTRODUCTION

It was never on the cards that the 1982 Test Matches would rival the previous summer's in drama and excitement. Double tours cannot work out that way. In addition, England and India had only just concluded the dreariest of encounters on the batting mattresses of India.

That was just part of it. No sooner had England returned from India than fifteen players, former, future, present or borderline Test cricketers, departed for South Africa, there to play a series of matches against a nominal South African Test side. The affair was sponsored by South African Breweries and the players, fully aware of the possible consequences, both to themselves and to their fellow professional cricketers, and in defiance of advice and agreements, lined their pockets satisfactorily. This squalid and furtively conducted adventure resulted in a three-year ban from Test cricket, the proper action of the T.C.C.B. in this matter being overwhelmingly endorsed by the cricketers' own Association.

For most of those concerned, the best of their careers was behind them and the ban was of little consequence. The exceptions, about whose absence great fuss was made, were Gooch and Emburey. Gooch, it should perhaps be recalled, averaged 13.9 against Australia in 1981 after 10 completed innings. Only at the very end of 1982 did he show anything like his old commanding form. Emburey certainly seemed a loss, though his 12 wickets against Australia cost 33.25 each and it is debatable whether he bowled any better in 1982 than Edmonds, his county colleague, who failed to hold his place in the England side.

There was also the little matter of the Falklands. For at least the first half of the season it was difficult to give proper attention to cricket when so absorbing and precarious an enterprise was being conducted elsewhere.

In the circumstances, the season of 1982 turned out surprisingly well. England beat both India and Pakistan, which was good for home morale, and in the second series there was scarcely a dull moment.

More than anything else, however, the summer was notable for the quite extraordinary all-round performances of Ian Botham, Kapil Dev and Imran Khan. Test class all-rounders come few and far between, in any case, but in all the Tests they played the achievements of these three were outstanding.

It was not, moreover, simply what they did but how they did it. All three are cricketers of magnetic skills, orthodox batsmen with immense hitting powers and bowlers of pace and swing. Kapil Dev and Botham carried out duels within a duel during the Indian Tests, and when England came to play Pakistan Imran Khan ousted even Botham from the limelight. Kapil Dev and Botham compare more easily, in that they are much of a muchness as bowlers and ferocious destroyers of attacks. Imran Khan is by some way the fastest bowler of the three and the more reserved batsman, but he carried his side even more nobly than, on occasions, did Kapil Dev and Botham theirs. It was the greatest of privileges that three such magnificent cricketers should have graced the fields of England in the same summer.

ENGLAND vs INDIA

LORD'S (10–15 June)

It took England only one match to remove the bad taste left by their defeat in India. During the winter India had won a low-scoring match in Bombay by 138 runs, Kapil Dev and Madan Lal bowling England out in their second innings for 102. The remaining five Tests – at Bangalore, Delhi, Calcutta, Madras, Kanpur – were played at a funereal tempo and never looked like producing the result England needed.

Fletcher, who led England in India, failed to impose himself sufficiently on either his own side or on the series. In consequence the selectors, under Peter May, their new Chairman, began to look elsewhere. To most people's surprise – and certainly his own – the choice fell on Bob Willis. Few fast bowlers have ever captained their country.

In the event, Willis had a good match, both as player and captain. He won the toss, made 28 runs, and took 3 for 41 and 6 for 101. England, batting first, lost three wickets for 37, but recovered to make 433. Randall scored 126, Botham 67 and Edmonds 64. In showery weather India lost 5 wickets for 45, mainly to Willis and Botham, but Kapil Dev, carrying on his blistering attack from the two one-day Prudential Tests, helped Gavaskar add 72. All out 128, India followed on. A patient and resourceful 157 from Vengsarkar – his second Test century at Lord's – and more terrific hitting by Kapil Dev restored much of their pride. Kapil Dev's 89 took only 55 balls and included three sixes and thirteen fours.

England needed only 65 to win, but Kapil Dev shot out Cook, Tavaré and Taylor for 18. Lamb, playing in his first Test, hit off the runs with Gower.

For once the tourists had travelled the counties in a warm, beautiful May. The moment the Tests started the weather broke, never properly recovering for the rest of the summer.

ENGLAND: First Innings

G. Cook, lbw, b Kapil Dev		4
C. J. Tavaré, c Viswanath, b Kapil Dev		4
A. J. Lamb, lbw, b Kapil Dev		9
D. I. Gower, c Viswanath, b Kapil Dev		37
I. T. Botham, c Malhotra, b Madan Lal		67
D. W. Randall, c Parkar, b Kapil Dev		126
D. R. Pringle, c Gavaskar, b Doshi		7
P. H. Edmonds, c Kirmani, b Madan Lal		64
R. W. Taylor, c Viswanath, b Doshi		31
P. J. W. Allott, not out		41
R. G. D. Willis, b Madan Lal		28
Extras (b 1, lb 5, nb 9)		15

TOTAL 433

Fall of Wickets: 1–5, 2–18, 3–37, 4–96, 5–149, 6–166, 7–291, 8–363, 9–363, 10–433.

Bowling: Kapil Dev, 43–8–125–5; Madan Lal, 28.1–6–99–3; Shastri, 34–10–73–0; Doshi, 40–7–120–2; Yashpal, 3–2–1–0.

INDIA: First Innings

S. M. Gavaskar, b Botham		48
G. A. Parkar, b Botham		6
D. B. Vengsarkar, lbw, b Willis		2
G. R. Viswanath, b Botham		1
Yashpal Sharma, lbw, b Pringle		4
A. Malhotra, lbw, b Pringle		5
Kapil Dev, c Cook, b Willis		41
R. J. Shastri, c Cook, b Willis		4
S. M. H. Kirmani, not out		6
Madan Lal, c Tavaré, b Botham		6
D. R. Doshi, c Taylor, b Botham		0
Extras (lb 1, nb 4)		5

TOTAL 128

Fall of Wickets: 1–17, 2–21, 3–22, 4–31, 5–45, 6–112, 7–116, 8–116, 9–128, 10–128.

Bowling: Botham, 19.4–3–46–5; Willis, 16–2–41–3; Pringle, 9–4–16–2; Edmonds, 2–1–15–0; Allott, 4–1–15–0.

INDIA: Second Innings

S. M. Gavaskar, c Cook, b Willis		24
G. A. Parkar, b Willis		1
D. B. Vengsarkar, c Allott, b Willis		157
R. J. Shastri, b Allott		23
G. R. Viswanath, c Taylor, b Pringle		3
Yashpal Sharma, b Willis		37
A. Malhotra, c Taylor, b Willis		0
Kapil Dev, c Cook, b Botham		89
S. M. H. Kirmani, c Gower, b Willis		3
Madan Lal, lbw, b Pringle		15
D. R. Doshi, not out		4
Extras (lb 2, nb 11)		13

TOTAL 369

Fall of Wickets: 1–6, 2–47, 3–107, 4–110, 5–252, 6–252, 7–254, 8–275, 9–341, 10–369.

Bowling: Botham, 31.5–7–103–1; Willis, 28–3–101–6; Pringle, 19–4–58–2; Edmonds, 15–6–39–0; Allott, 17–3–51–1; Cook, 1–0–4–0.

ENGLAND: Second Innings

G. Cook, lbw, b Kapil Dev		10
C. J. Tavaré, b Kapil Dev		3
R. W. Taylor, c Malhotra, b Kapil Dev		1
A. J. Lamb, not out		37
D. I. Gower, not out		14
Extras (lb 2)		2

TOTAL 67

I. T. Botham, D. W. Randall, D. R. Pringle, P. H. Edmonds, P. J. W. Allott and R. G. D. Willis did not bat.

Fall of Wickets: 1–11, 2–13, 3–18.

Bowling: Kapil Dev, 10–1–43–3; Madan Lal, 2–1–2–0; Shastri, 2–0–9–0; Doshi, 5–3–11–0.

Umpires: D. G. L. Evans and B. J. Meyer.

England won by 7 wkts.

Cook was an obvious choice in the absence of Gooch and Boycott. Kapil Dev had him lbw

LEFT Botham swings Yashpal Sharma to leg during his innings of 67. Botham was soon experimenting in county matches with a reverse sweep, despatching the ball past slip. The fielder at short leg has no choice but to take evasive action. Too many players were hit in these suicidally close positions, the benefits of which remain doubtful. Ted Dexter, in a thoughtful article in the September *Wisden Cricket Monthly*, argued that they did spin bowlers more harm than good, Edmonds and Qadir in particular, by discouraging flighted spin in favour of flat skidding trajectory. Dexter advocated a six-yard fielder-free zone in front of the wicket, and no protective gear for fielders, other than the wicket-keeper. It is an idea worth following up, and would have saved Gavaskar unpleasant injury in the last Test.

BELOW LEFT Edmonds during his innings of 64. He lost his place against Pakistan after taking only 6 wickets in three Tests against India.

RIGHT Taylor batted nearly two hours for an invaluable 31. In match after match Taylor, with his resolute defence and occasional square cuts, proved difficult to shift. Behind the stumps he was as safe as ever.

BELOW RIGHT Willis has many interesting strokes, but he probably had to chalk his cue after this one. Or is he taking aim at a Lord's seagull? Although Willis found wickets hard to come by for Warwickshire at Edgbaston, his batting flourished. He made 72 against the Indians, his first fifty in first-class cricket, and also his first championship fifty, 63 not out against Gloucestershire. As a bowler, he sensibly reserved his best efforts for Test matches. In this innings he added 70 with Allott for the last wicket.

Pringle in his first Test match took 2 for 16 and 2 for 58. The first undergraduate to represent England since Peter May, Pringle vexed University purists by preferring to play for England at Old Trafford instead of leading Cambridge at Lord's. In 1981 Pringle had a top score for Essex of 28 and took 10 wickets in the championship at 55.4 each.

He was picked on promise rather than performance, though he enjoyed an exceptionally prolific start to the season at Fenners. Nairobi-born and over 6′4″, Pringle played for Cambridge 1979–82. His height gives him bounce when others sometimes fail to find it. Something seems odd about his left leg in this picture, as if he were going in two directions at once. But such an eccentricity is not normally noticeable. He did not make much impact on the summer's Tests, averaging only 13 against India and taking 7 wickets at 31.29 each. Thereafter injury, once from stretching himself after writing a letter on the eve of the Third Test against Pakistan, prevented him from doing himself justice.

ABOVE Yashpal Sharma lbw Pringle 4. There would not seem to be much doubt about Pringle's first Test wicket.

Randall in an unselfconscious act of exposure happily not often seen at Lord's. In this instance a thigh pad had come adrift, not surprisingly, with all the twitching and fidgeting to which all Randall's equipment is subjected. Randall batted nearly six hours for his 126, hitting one six and eleven fours. He made 0 in the Second Test, 95 in the Third, finishing second to Botham with an average of 73. Pressed into duty as an opener against Pakistan, he made 17 and 105 at Edgbaston, but the experiment was sensibly not pursued after two uneasy performances at Lord's. His fielding and general enthusiasm, no less than his puppet-like restlessness at the wicket, meant it was never dull when he was on view.

LEFT Against England in India, Sunil Gavaskar, India's compact and handsome captain, made 500 runs, with an average of 62. At the Oval in 1979 he made 221 against England, an innings which those who saw it will never forget. In that Test he put on 213 with Chauhan for the first wicket, an Indian record for England–India Tests, as was his aggregate of 542, average 77, in that series. Despite his superb playing of Willis at Lord's, his technique masterly in so small a man against Willis's steep lift, he managed only 74 runs in his three Test innings in 1982.

BELOW Vengsarkar has a taste for Lord's. Of the 193 runs he made in 5 Test innings, 157 were made in this one innings at Lord's. His hooking and dismissive strokes off the back foot were especially notable.

LEFT Kirmani, c Gower, b Willis 3. The English slips form an unusually jagged arc, Botham standing so oddly in relation to Pringle that it would seem that his left arm and Pringle's right cover much the same ground. For once Taylor's hat – of the kind associated with lady bowls players or curate's wives at vicarage tea parties – is the only one of its kind visible. In county matches they comfortably outnumber caps.

BELOW LEFT Edmonds adds his own particular version to this picture, a white bowler similar in shape to those worn by Peruvian peasant women. He only parts with it reluctantly.

RIGHT Kapil Dev hooking Willis during his innings of 89. He could probably do it equally well off the other leg, or no leg at all.

LEFT The end of the match, and two Northamptonshire colleagues, Allan Lamb and Kapil Dev, shake on it. Lamb, with 9 and 37 not out, had mixed fortunes, though he made up for it with a maiden Test century at the Oval in the Third Test. His class, despite several failures, was never in doubt. For Kapil Dev his 41 and 89 were the first salvos of an extraordinary campaign that brought him 65 in 77 minutes at Old Trafford, and 97 in 105 minutes at the Oval. He ended with an average of 73 and took 10 wickets at 43 apiece.

RIGHT There could only really have been one man of the match. 41 and 89, 5 for 125 and 3 for 43 takes some beating, but Botham 67, 5 for 46 and 1 for 103, Willis with 9 wickets, Randall 126, and Vengsarkar 157 all had claims.

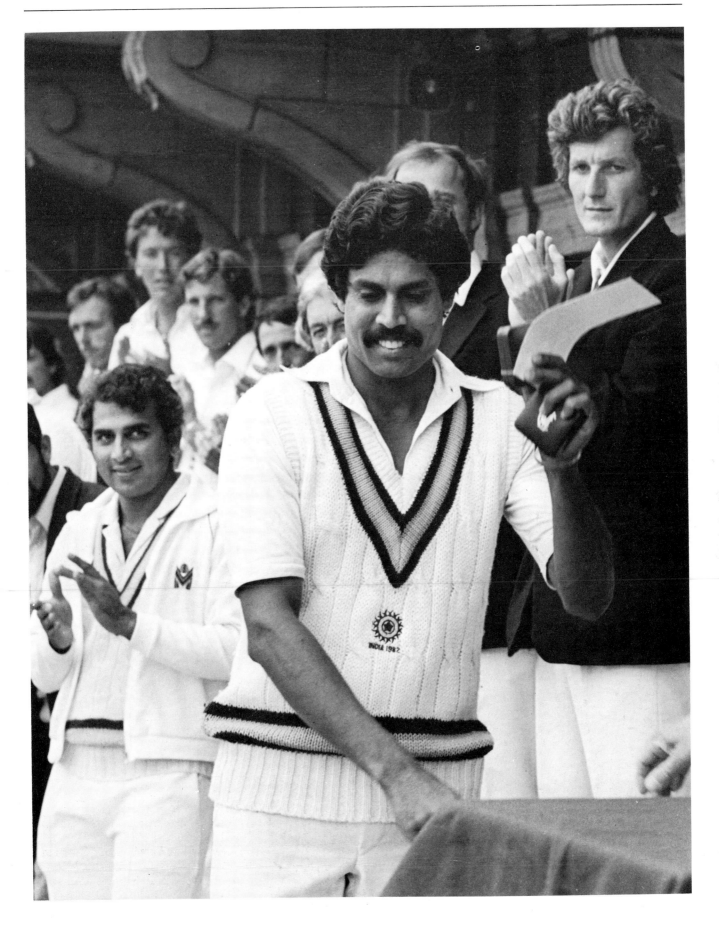

ENGLAND vs INDIA

SECOND TEST

OLD TRAFFORD (24–28 June)

As against the Australians last year, rain took the heart out of the Second Test. This time not even two innings could be completed. It was not all loss, though, for despite the weather and disappointing crowds, there were several splendid individual performances. Botham scored 128 in little over three hours, Miller made 98, his highest and most accomplished Test innings, and for India Patil, after an incomprehensibly wretched six weeks, lashed the England bowlers all over Old Trafford. There was little to be got out of the game by then, but it was a glorious innings all the same, and in the course of it Patil hit Willis for six fours in one, albeit seven ball, over. Doshi, too, bowled beautifully, taking 6 for 102 in 47 overs.

India facing an England total of 425, batted with such spirit after losing Gavaskar, Shastri and Vengsarkar for 25, that they ended up 379 for 8. There was no play at all on the last day.

ENGLAND: First Innings

G. Cook, b Doshi	66
C. J. Tavaré, b Doshi	57
A. J. Lamb, c Viswanath, b Madan Lal	9
D. I. Gower, c Shastri, b Madan Lal	9
I. T. Botham, b Shastri	128
D. W. Randall, c Kirmani, b Doshi	0
G. Miller, c Vengsarkar, b Doshi	98
D. R. Pringle, st Kirmani, b Doshi	23
P. H. Edmonds, c Kirmani, b Madan Lal	12
R. W. Taylor, not out	1
R. G. D. Willis, c Gavaskar, b Doshi	6
Extras (b 2, lb 5, nb 9)	16

TOTAL 425

Fall of Wickets: 1–106, 2–117, 3–141, 4–161, 5–161, 6–330, 7–382, 8–413, 9–419, 10–425.

Bowling: Kapil Dev, 36–5–109–0; Madan Lal, 35–9–104–3; Nayak, 12–1–50–0; Doshi, 47.1–17–102–6; Shastri, 23–8–44–1.

INDIA: First Innings

S. M. Gavaskar, c Tavaré, b Willis	2
R. J. Shastri, c Cook, b Willis	0
D. B. Vengsarkar, c Randall, b Pringle	12
G. R. Viswanath, c Taylor, b Botham	54
S. M. H. Kirmani, b Edmonds	58
Yashpal Sharma, b Edmonds	10
S. M. Patil, not out	129
Kapil Dev, c Taylor, b Miller	65
Madan Lal, b Edmonds	26
A. V. Nayak, not out	2
Extras (b 6, lb 2, w 3, nb 10)	21

TOTAL (8 wkts) 379

D. R. Doshi did not bat.

Fall of Wickets: 1–5, 2–8, 3–25, 4–112, 5–136, 6–173, 7–269, 8–366.

Bowling: Willis, 17–2–94–2; Pringle, 15–4–33–1; Edmonds, 37–12–94–3; Botham, 19–4–86–1; Miller, 16–4–51–1.

Umpires: H. D. Bird and B. J. Meyer.

Match drawn.

Kapil Dev took 0 for 109 in this innings, but there was nothing wrong with his aggression or his stamina. Cook and Tavaré, on a cold cloudy morning, blunted the new ball attack with an opening partnership of 106, after which five wickets fell for 55, three of them to Doshi.

It was a pitch rather more suited to the guile and patience of Doshi than the energetic thrust of Kapil Dev, who, later in the day, took some stick from Botham.

LEFT Cook falls to Doshi for 66.

BELOW Doshi has the look of someone addressing a conspiratorial meeting on the maidan in Calcutta, but he is in fact explaining how he hypnotised Randall into losing his wicket third ball. Randall drew back to cut but instead edged the ball to the wicket-keeper.

RIGHT Miller, yet to score a first-class hundred, deserved one this time. Once before, against Pakistan in 1977/8, he reached 98, and now, pushing out at Doshi, he was caught close in by Vengsarkar two runs short of his hundred. Miller had a dismal season in 1981, which included relinquishing the captaincy of Derbyshire. He averaged 19 with the bat, and took only 33 wickets with his off-spinners.

A change for the better was immediately noticeable in his all-round play at the start of this season, and his batting in this innings, crisply confident, confirmed it. What Kirmani lacks on top of his head he makes up for under it.

LEFT Shastri, pressed into service as an opening batsman, made no runs, but he bowled 23 overs and took the wicket of Botham for 44 runs. Gavaskar points to the blade of grass onto which he wants the ball pitched.

RIGHT Botham, more used to dishing it out, is here on the receiving end. The stout boots worn in earlier days would have protected him.

BELOW RIGHT This looks like going for four, but the ball spun via his feet onto his stumps. This was Botham's second successive Test century at Old Trafford. He hit two sixes and nineteen fours.

LEFT Gavaskar, so skilled at dropping rising balls like stunned mullet at his feet, could not keep this one down, and Tavaré took a sharp catch at second slip.

BELOW LEFT Patil drives and Miller deflects the ball onto the stumps. But the batsman is not out.

RIGHT Viswanath averaged 58 against England during the winter and hit two hundreds. His highest score in this series was 75 not out, but without ever dominating he still averaged 47. Here, he has been hit by Willis who looks as if he may have forgotten to renew his insurance. Viswanath batted only 110 minutes for 54, hitting eight fours, mainly through the covers.

Edmonds took 3 for 94 in 37 overs, and in this picture he has bowled Yashpal Sharma for 10 with one of several that kept low. At 126 for 5 Patil arrived. He lost Kirmani at 173, Edmonds bowling him with one that turned off a length to beat his back stroke. For the rest of the day, first with Kapil Dev, then with Madan Lal, Patil showed what a high-class batsman he is at his best. There was no stroke he did not play, and his timing was such that most of his 18 boundaries required no chase from the fielders. Here he has struck Miller for six, swinging himself off his feet in Kanhai fashion. Patil played only two innings in the series, scoring 191 for once out.

BELOW This time both Pringle's legs seem to be pointing in the same direction and his determination is evident. He made 23 runs and took 1 for 33, opening the bowling with Willis while Botham nursed his toe. His reward was the wicket of Vengsarkar, caught off a careless stroke at fourth slip for 12.

RIGHT Even Taylor seems to wince at the power of this stroke from Kapil Dev. His 65, including one six and nine fours, took only 77 minutes. His batting gloves have the look of Indian bananas.

No-one can get any pleasure out of a scene like this, except possibly the manufacturers of Jager lager and Vladivar vodka, and the Bradford & Bingley and Skipton Building Societies.

ENGLAND vs INDIA

THIRD TEST

THE OVAL (8–13 July)

The series ended tamely enough, but not before there had been a devastating double century by Botham, an assured hundred by Lamb and several fine innings by the Indians, Kapil Dev, Patil and Viswanath in particular.

Willis won the toss for the third time in succession, and by the end of the second day England had amassed 594. When Botham came in the score was 185 for 3, Tavaré having gone for 39, Cook for 50, and Gower for 47.

Botham battled for 276 minutes, hitting four sixes and nineteen fours in one of the most brilliant attacking innings ever played. The only reservation possible about it was the comparatively modest nature of the bowling. The pitch, after heavy rain, was docile, and an attack comprising Kapil Dev, Madan Lal, Nayak, Doshi, and Shastri was unlikely to intimidate.

Nevertheless, Botham reduced so fluent a player as Lamb to almost a sleeping partner. They batted virtually the same length of time – Botham 16 minutes longer – and Botham scored twice as many runs.

Randall played another useful innings, and at one stage England were 512 for 4. India went in needing 395 to save the follow-on. They were without Gavaskar, his ankle broken when fielding at silly point to Botham, but they managed it with 7 wickets down. A hurricane 97 by Kapil Dev, much in the Botham idiom, was mainly responsible, but everyone except Vengsarkar contributed.

Willis allowed England to bat on too long, or rather too boringly, on the last day. He eventually declared at 191 for 3, setting India 376 to win at about nine an over. They ambled gently along to 111 for 3.

No other result was probably possible, but livelier, more imaginative batting earlier in the day would have given Willis at least some glimpse of the possibilities and the Oval faithful a better return for their money.

ENGLAND: First Innings

G. Cook, c Shastri, b Patil		50
C. J. Tavaré, b Kapil Dev		39
A. J. Lamb, run out		107
D. I. Gower, c Kirmani, b Shastri		47
I. T. Botham, c Viswanath, b Doshi		208
D. W. Randall, st Kirmani, b Shastri		95
D. R. Pringle, st Kirmani, b Doshi		9
P. H. Edmonds, c sub (Parkar), b Doshi		14
R. W. Taylor, lbw, b Shastri		3
P. W. J. Allott, c Sharma, b Doshi		3
R. G. D. Willis, not out		1
Extras (b 3, lb 5, nb 10)		18

TOTAL 594

Fall of Wickets: 1–96, 2–96, 3–185, 4–361, 5–512, 6–534, 7–562, 8–569, 9–581, 10–594.

Bowling: Kapil Dev, 25–4–109–1; Madan Lal, 26–8–69–0; Nayak, 21–5–66–0; Patil, 14–1–48–1; Doshi, 46–6–175–4; Shastri, 41.3–8–109–3.

INDIA: First Innings

R. J. Shastri, c Botham, b Willis		66
D. B. Vengsarkar, c Edmonds, b Botham		6
G. R. Viswanath, lbw, b Willis		56
Yashpal Sharma, c Gower, b Willis		38
S. M. Patil, c sub (N. R. Taylor), b Botham		62
S. M. H. Kirmani, b Allott		43
Kapil Dev, c Allott, b Edmonds		97
Madan Lal, c Taylor, b Edmonds		5
S. V. Nayak, b Edmonds		11
D. R. Doshi, not out		5
Extras (b 3, lb 5, nb 13)		21

TOTAL 410

S. M. Gavaskar absent hurt.

Fall of Wickets: 1–21, 2–134, 3–135, 4–232, 5–248, 6–378, 7–394, 8–396, 9–410.

Bowling: Willis, 23–4–78–3; Botham, 19–2–73–2; Allott, 24–4–69–1; Pringle, 28–5–80–0; Edmonds, 35.2–11–89–3.

ENGLAND: Second Innings

G. Cook, c Sharma, b Kapil Dev		8
C. J. Tavaré, not out		75
A. J. Lamb, b Doshi		45
D. I. Gower, c & b Nayak		45
Extras (b 6, lb 8, nb 4)		18

TOTAL (3 wkts dec) 191

I. T. Botham, D. W. Randall, D. R. Pringle, P. H. Edmonds, R. W. Taylor, P. W. J. Allott, and R. G. D. Willis did not bat.

Fall of Wickets: 1–12, 2–94, 3–191.

Bowling: Kapil Dev, 19–3–53–1; Madan Lal, 11–6–17–0; Doshi, 19–5–47–1; Shastri, 16–3–40–0; Nayak, 5.3–0–16–1.

INDIA: Second Innings

R. J. Shastri, c Taylor, b Willis		0
S. V. Nayak, c Taylor, b Pringle		6
D. B. Vengsarkar, c Taylor, b Pringle		16
G. R. Viswanath, not out		75
Yashpal Sharma, not out		9
Extras (lb 3, nb 2)		5

TOTAL (3 wkts) 111

S. M. Patil, S. M. H. Kirmani, Kapil Dev, Madan Lal and D. R. Doshi did not bat. S. M. Gavaskar absent hurt.

Fall of Wickets: 1–0, 2–18, 3–43.

Bowling: Willis, 4–0–16–1; Pringle, 11–5–32–2; Edmonds, 13–5–34–0; Allott, 4–1–12–0; Botham, 4–0–12–0.

Umpires: H. D. Bird and A. G. T. Whitehead.

Match drawn.

The news seems serious. A leak in the dressing room? A defector among the Selectors? *Gay News* found in the Umpire's hut? Probably nothing of the kind. But Willis provides a jacuzzi of journalists from agencies, and the popular Press, with something to write about, even if it's only Botham's big toe.

Willis voiced some bitter complaints about the Press after England's victory at Headingley last year. Perhaps he knows better now, or at least knows enough to keep quiet about it.

Players often resent, with good reason, what seems to them media disloyalty; but, generally speaking, they get praise when they deserve it, criticism when they don't. Some only appreciate the former.

LEFT Allan Lamb wanted a hundred in this match, and, after a deliberate start – he was forty minutes on 1 – he got it. It was his bad luck that so assured a maiden Test century should have been acquired in the shadow of Botham. As this picture shows, Lamb's technique is correct, bat always close to the body when it should be. He is quick on his feet, too, a neat, all-round player who can hook, cut and drive with the best of them. South African-born, he learned his cricket in the Cape. It is ironic that in a season when 15 English-born players forfeited their right to play for England, a South African – until of late – should have qualified to do so.

BELOW Another blossoming innings nipped in the bud. Gower was cruising elegantly along when he went to steer Shastri and was caught at the wicket for 47. It says something for his consistency, and also for his fallibility, that with a top score of 47 he should still have averaged 38.

LEFT Botham driving off the back foot, head still and the bat following perfectly in the direction of the ball. Botham's promotion to No. 5 in the order marked the recognition of a mature Test batsman. His batting throughout the summer was classic in its breeding, the full face of the bat shown to the ball and the judgement of length impeccable. He was no less exciting to watch than when he scattered spectators from lower in the order.

BELOW His bruised toe needed air and freedom, like its owner. A full toss in the same place doesn't bear thinking about.

RIGHT Gavaskar pays the penalty for his foolhardiness. A sad end to his tour, but fielding so close to a batsman like Botham, on a pitch of this kind, is asking for trouble.

LEFT Botham looks pavilion-
ward at reaching 200. Birds and
fishes must fear that poacher's
grin. Randall actually seems to
be standing still.

ABOVE AND BELOW The reverse
sweep, variously executed. A
joke, show-off shot, whose
fashion may last about as long as
Colin Cowdrey's paddle or punk
haircuts. Botham has scored runs
with it and also missed some.
When it fails it looks plain silly.

BELOW Not some obscure Tantric rite or meditative ritual, but Kirmani adjusting his finger-stall. No friend to hairdressers, Kirmani makes a good foil to his colleagues with their lush, dark locks.

BOTTOM One of a hundred ways of getting out of bed, strengthening stomach muscles, increasing potency or catching a lobster. Shastri's boots have had enough of fielding.

BELOW RIGHT Groucho Marx once visited Lord's on the third day of a Middlesex–Cambridge match. The spectators consisted of a man in the Warner Stand and a girl in the Grand Stand.

Standing up in his check suit and gesturing at the two with his cigar, he bellowed out: 'Say, why don't you two get together?' It could only be Indians under those umbrellas on a sunny day.

LEFT Patil cuts, Lamb shimmies:
a cute version of the Oval
Charleston. For all he could do
about it Lamb might have gone
the way of Gavaskar. Who will
be next?

BELOW LEFT Botham testing the
wicket for nuclear fall-out. Or
has he detected marijuana?
Actually Edmonds has grazed
Nayak's stumps but a breeze
from the East has kept the bails
glued.

RIGHT Whatever Botham did,
Kapil Dev usually managed to
show that he could do it too.
When did two such great
magnetic all-rounders last grace
the same series?

BELOW Doshi bowled 65 overs in the match and took 5 wickets for, well, let us say plenty. If it had not been for his various marathon stints, Kapil Dev would not have had the energy to hit fours, let alone sixes. He might look, behind his specs, like a French philosopher/novelist, but all his guiles are aeronautical, not linguistic.

BELOW RIGHT Dickie Bird, under his flat white cap, might grin like a cat with a succulent mouse in view, but Shastri had to wheel away for almost as long as Doshi. He bowled 57 overs and took 3 for 149. He is an all-rounder with a future.

BELOW Everyone knows, or
ought to know by now, that
Tavaré can do it when he tries.
But why, occupying the crease
for so long, does he not get on
with it earlier? The gardens of St
John's College, Oxford, ought to
have inculcated a more serene
state of mind.

ABOVE England's slip field to Willis. Botham, against Pakistan, was more than once slow in getting down from so upright a position and catches went begging. But if you've bowled most of the day, and batted half the previous one, it's certainly excusable. Perhaps there's a case though, for letting him rest elsewhere. Sometimes he still catches blinders.

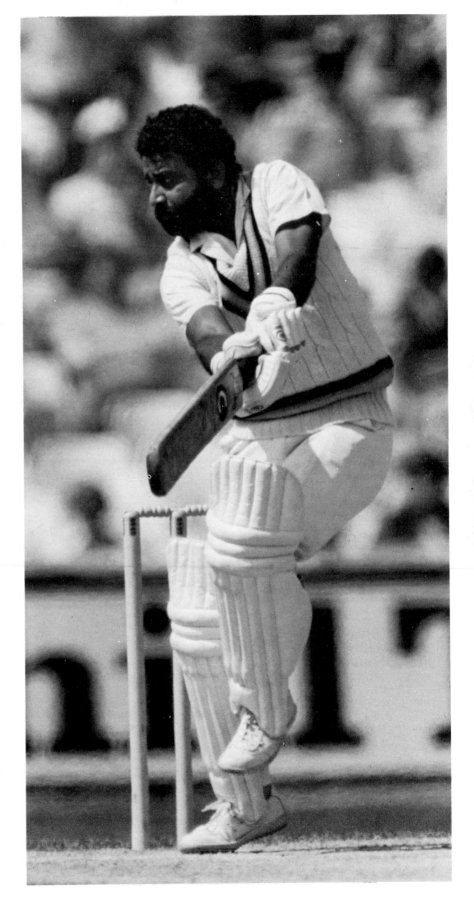

RIGHT Fakirs eating live fire or on beds of nails sometimes bear as fraught an expression, but Viswanath has kept this one down somehow. His 56 and 75 not out were delightful innings, but he was not, in the series, a force to be reckoned with.

Botham signs off, for the
moment. The Indian master, in
plaster, may have had his day.
India lost, mainly because they
had no real pace in their attack.
Had Willis changed sides it could
have been a different story. For
India, the form of Kapil Dev,
Patil, and Vengsarkar should
have made up for disappoint-
ments. India always had to bat
second and face large totals, but
from their second innings at
Lord's they showed a spirit and
resourcefulness often absent in
the predecessors.

ENGLAND vs PAKISTAN

FIRST TEST

EDGBASTON (29 July–1 August)

For all their moments of charm and salvoes of individual brilliance the Indians never really took hold of the imagination as a team. It was generally expected that Pakistan, individually rather more gifted as batsmen, and backed up with the fast bowling of Imran Khan and the leg-spin of Abdul Qadir, would prove a much tougher proposition. And so it proved, though not quite in the way expected.

For example, Zaheer Abbas, massive scorer in all other engagements, was never quite himself in the Tests and his impact was negligible. Sarfraz, generally unfit, bowled only 37 overs. As a result, Pakistan only once – at Lords – batted anything like up to their potential and their bowling never fired on all cylinders. Curiously, two of their least fancied bowlers, Mudassar Nazar and Tahir Naqqash, caused England on occasion real trouble.

Nevertheless, it was an absorbing series, from first to last, and it was one that Pakistan, heroically led for the first time by Imran Khan, could well have won. They suffered, in one or two vital instances, from unfortunate umpiring decisions, but they had the winning of the First Test in their hands, only to throw it away by reckless and undisciplined batting.

Deservedly they won the Second Test by 10 wickets, after which they should have been able to go home happy. Instead they had merely drawn level.

The decider, at Headingley, could scarcely have been more closely contested. Only 19 runs – in Pakistan's favour – separated the sides after the first innings, but Pakistan's second innings collapse to Willis and Botham, when they lost their first seven wickets for 128, gave them too few runs to play with. England, wanting 219 to win, went from 103 for no wicket to 199 for 7, but squeaked home in the end without further loss.

Disappointed though Pakistan were – with the result, themselves, and the umpiring, not necessarily in that order – there could be no doubt at all about the performance of their captain. Imran Khan dominated every match. He took more wickets than anyone else on either side (and bowled the most overs) and he averaged 53 with the bat, only Mohsin Khan and Tavaré scoring more. Botham in the series scored 163 at an average of 27.16, Imran 212 at an average of 53; Botham took 18 wickets at 26.55

ENGLAND: First Innings

D. W. Randall, b Imran	17
C. J. Tavaré, c Miandad, b Qadir	54
A. J. Lamb, c Wasim Bari, b Sikander	6
D. I. Gower, c Wasim Bari, b Imran	74
I. T. Botham, b Imran	2
M. W. Gatting, b Tahir	17
G. Miller, b Imran	47
I. A. Greig, c sub (Haroon Rashid), b Imran	14
E. E. Hemmings, lbw, b Imran	2
R. W. Taylor, lbw, b Imran	1
R. G. D. Willis, not out	0
Extras (b 4, lb 10, w 6, nb 18)	38
TOTAL	272

Fall of Wickets: 1–29, 2–37, 3–164, 4–172, 5–179, 6–228, 7–263, 8–265, 9–271, 10–272.

Bowling: Imran, 25.3–11–52–7; Tahir, 15–4–46–1; Sikander, 18–5–58–1; Mudassar, 5–2–8–0; Qadir, 29–7–70–1.

PAKISTAN: First Innings

Mudassar Nazar, lbw, b Botham	0
Mohsin Khan, c Willis, b Botham	26
Tahir Naqqash, c Taylor, b Greig	12
Mansoor Akhtar, c Miller, b Hemmings	58
Javed Miandad, c Willis, b Hemmings	30
Zaheer Abbas, lbw, b Greig	40
Wasim Raja, c Tavaré, b Willis	26
Imran Khan, c Taylor, b Willis	22
Wasim Bari, not out	16
Abdul Qadir, lbw, b Greig	7
Sikander Bakht, c Hemmings, b Greig	1
Extras (b 5, lb 2, w 1, nb 5)	13
TOTAL	251

Fall of Wickets: 1–0, 2–29, 3–53, 4–110, 5–164, 6–198, 7–217, 8–227, 9–248, 10–251.

Bowling: Botham, 24–4–86–2; Greig, 14.2–3–53–4; Willis, 15–3–42–2; Hemmings, 24–5–56–2; Miller, 2–1–1–0.

ENGLAND: Second Innings

D. W. Randall, b Imran	105
C. J. Tavaré, c Mohsin, b Imran	17
A. J. Lamb, lbw, b Tahir	5
D. I. Gower, c Mudassar, b Tahir	13
M. W. Gatting, c Wasim Bari, b Tahir	5
I. T. Botham, lbw, b Tahir	0
G. Miller, b Tahir	5
I. A. Greig, b Qadir	7
E. E. Hemmings, c Mansoor, b Qadir	19
R. W. Taylor, c Qadir, b Wasim Raja	54
R. G. D. Willis, not out	28
Extras (b 10, lb 11, w 7, nb 5)	33
TOTAL	291

Fall of Wickets: 1–62, 2–98, 3–127, 4–137, 5–137, 6–146, 7–170, 8–188, 9–212, 10–291.

Bowling: Imran Khan, 32–5–84–2; Sikander, 13–5–34–0; Abdul Qadir, 40–10–100–2; Tahir, 18–7–40–5; Wasim Raja, 2.3–2–0–1.

PAKISTAN: Second Innings

Mudassar Nazar, lbw, b Botham	0
Mohsin Khan, lbw, b Botham	35
Mansoor Akhtar, c Taylor, b Botham	0
Javed Miandad, run out	10
Zaheer Abbas, c Taylor, b Willis	4
Wasim Raja, c Gower, b Willis	16
Imran Khan, b Miller	65
Wasim Bari, c Taylor, b Botham	12
Tahir Naqqash, c & b Hemmings	39
Abdul Qadir, c Randall, b Miller	9
Sikander Bakht, not out	1
Extras (lb 3, nb 5)	8
TOTAL	199

Fall of Wickets: 1–0, 2–0, 3–38, 4–54, 5–66, 6–77, 7–98, 8–151, 9–178, 10–199.

Bowling: Botham, 21–7–70–4; Willis, 14–2–49–2; Greig, 4–1–19–0; Hemmings, 10–4–27–1; Miller, 7.4–1–26–2.

Umpires: D. G. L. Evans and K. E. Palmer.

England won by 113 runs.

Imran's racing approach and whippy, leaping delivery are one of the glories of the contemporary game. In earlier days something of a slinger, with inadequate control, he has developed into a shrewd and exciting bowler, as quick when flat out as anyone now bowling. He showed in these matches remarkable stamina, and he proved himself master of most of the pace bowler's arts. He had to – or chose to – bowl too much, but he was the only consistently threatening bowler Pakistan had.

LEFT Randall made 17 and 105 in the match, and Imran bowled him both times. In this picture, after a perky start, he has unaccountably played no stroke to a ball slanted in from wide of the crease. The bail, despite appearances, is not being spat out.

RIGHT Botham managed only 2 and 0, a rare double failure. This was his sixth ball, from Imran, and it hit the base of the off stump. Perhaps the hat did it, obscuring normal vision. At any rate, Botham looks put out. His second innings lasted only one ball.

LEFT One of Gower's many serene and silken strokes in his first innings of 74. Miandad claimed to have caught him at slip when he was 24 but the appeal was refused, a decision Miandad appeared to regard only as the basis for negotiation.

RIGHT The opinion seems general that Tavaré ought to go, but he did not. Tavaré was only on view $4\frac{1}{4}$ hours for 54, but long enough to show he was more comfortable against pace than spin.

BELOW RIGHT Gower this time *is* out, touching a beauty from Imran that left him. Wasim Bari took several fine catches but was not agile enough to get across to sometimes erratic bowling. The extras in England's six innings were 38, 33, 46, 38, 24, 42.

BELOW Not for the only time the ball causes problems. Mohsin is upset at not being shown a replacement while Evans and Palmer compare specimens like a couple of fruiterers at the market.

LEFT Shame on those who put up such silly banners, too. Mohsin, no doubt distracted, flings his bat at this one and (out of your picture, as they say) is caught by Willis.

LEFT Javed Miandad, one of four ex-captains on the party, was caught off this stroke, having played a similarly risky one the ball before. The bowler was Hemmings, who bowled tidily to take 2 for 56 in 24 overs. Miandad paid the penalty for a general air of cockiness, misplaced more often than was good for his side.

RIGHT Imran batted at seven, which was too low for him. In the end he was carrying the batting as well as the bowling, getting his head down in a fashion his predecessors cared to do only intermittently.

Randall's second innings 105 was combative and crisp, even though he looked often against Qadir to have but the sketchiest notion of where the ball was coming from or going to. Nevertheless, he struck eleven fours in a determined innings of over 4 hours. He was eighth out at 188, the invisible strings to which, like a puppet, he cheerfully jerks and dances, rather less in evidence.

England in their second innings got off to a start of 62 before a wicket fell. The medium-paced Tahir Naqqash, playing only because of Sarfraz's unfitness, then reduced them to 212 for 9, taking 5 for 40 in 18 overs. Willis and Taylor added 79 for the last wicket, the biggest stand of the innings. Taylor, who batted nearly 3 hours for 54, latches on to a short one from Qadir (*left*); *below left*, Willis pads one away with the hauteur of an émigré grandee refusing a dish, while Qadir vents his wrath on the chef; Taylor skips out of the firing line (*right*) and Willis, slyly immune in the previous picture, gets a taste of the same medicine from Sikander Bakht.

Pakistan, needing 313 to win, made a disastrous start, losing two wickets for 0. Botham, who had Mudassar lbw second ball, has just had Mansoor caught at the wicket with his sixth ball. Mudassar, averaging 291 against the counties in the run-up to the Tests, failed to score in the match. Pakistan continued to lose wickets and at 98 for 7 had lost all hope. Botham, on a hazy morning, swung the ball towards the slips and Willis banged it in at a high cld pace. Tavaré, here looking more animated than ever he does when batting, seems to be conducting a gentle waltz between Botham and Miller, with Randall the wallflower.

LEFT Mansoor, after a confident 58 in the first innings, has edged one to Taylor. It could be the Notting Hill Carnival, but the music is Botham, not reggae.

BELOW LEFT Gatting, sadly disappointing with the bat, has made a fine stop at short leg and flicked the ball in to run out a startled Miandad.

RIGHT Imran batted patiently until the very end, despite the blissful exuberance of his partners, Tahir especially, who ignored every signal to be careful and acquired 39 in little over half an hour. When all was finally lost, Imran drove Hemmings for two soaring sixes, being last out for 65.

BELOW Randall was in action for most of the last three days, and fielding, close in or in the covers, contrives to be as much a part of the narrative as the bowler or the batsman.

RIGHT Here he makes a superb catch off Miller, diving to pick off Qadir via bat and pad.

BELOW RIGHT The match is won and if anyone deserves to celebrate it is Randall. His Test days looked to be over, but, pitchforked into opening the innings, he did well enough to earn a passage to Australia. Lamb, with an average of 8 after six innings against Pakistan, learned something about failure.

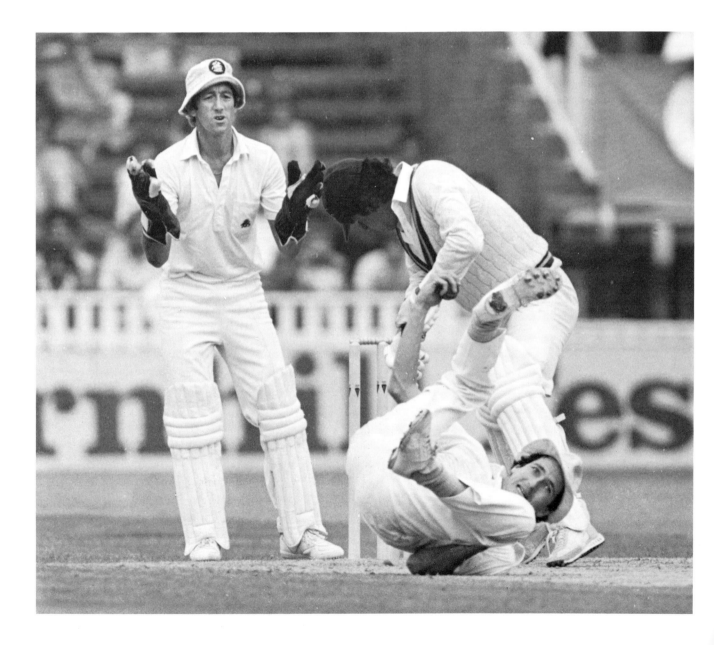

ENGLAND vs PAKISTAN

SECOND TEST

LORD'S (12–16 August)

Only once – in 1954 – had Pakistan won a Test match in England and that was when Fazal Mahmood bowled them to victory at the Oval against a voluntarily experimental England side. This time they won in great style and in the grand manner at the best place of all. In the last resort, held up by Taylor and Jackman, they had to make 76 off a possible 18 overs to win. They did it with 4.2 overs to spare and without losing a wicket.

Willis, suffering from a stiff neck, was unable to play and Gower captained England. Seldom have England fielded a milder pace attack, and there was no left-arm spinner to give the bowling variety.

In neither innings, on a lovely batting wicket, did England bat as they should have done. Qadir, after Sarfraz had removed Randall and Tavaré, foxed all the later batsmen in the first innings, and the gentle paced Mudassar, drifting the ball in from the extreme edge of the crease, took 6 for 32 in the second innings.

For Pakistan, Mohsin Khan played a glorious, euphoric innings of 200, launching himself like an eagle at the bowling.

PAKISTAN: First Innings

Mohsin Khan, c Tavaré, b Jackman 200
Mudassar Nazat, c Taylor, b Jackman 20
Mansoor Akhtar, c Lamb, b Botham 57
Javed Miandad, run out 6
Zaheer Abbas, b Jackman 75
Haroon Rashid, lbw, b Botham 1
Imran Khan, c Taylor, b Botham 12
Tahir Naqqash, c Gatting, b Jackman 2
Wasim Bari, not out 24
Abdul Qadir, not out 18
Extras (b 3, lb 8, nb 2) 13

TOTAL (8 wkts dec) 428

Sarfraz Nawaz did not bat.

Fall of Wickets: 1–53, 2–197, 3–208, 4–361, 5–364, 6–380, 7–382, 8–401.

Bowling: Botham, 44–8–148–3; Jackman, 36–5–110–4; Pringle, 26–9–62–0; Greig, 13–2–42–0; Hemmings, 20–3–53–0.

ENGLAND: First Innings

D. W. Randall, b Sarfraz 29
C. J. Tavaré, b Sarfraz 8
A. J. Lamb, c Haroon, b Tahir 33
D. I. Gower, c Mansoor, b Imran 29
I. T. Botham, c Moshin, b Qadir 31
M. W. Gatting, not out 32
D. R. Pringle, c Haroon, b Qadir 5
I. A. Greig, lbw, b Qadir 3
E. E. Hemmings, b Sarfraz 6
R. W. Taylor, lbw, b Qadir 5
R. D. Jackman, lbw, b Imran 0
Extras (b 11, lb 12, w 13, nb 10) 46

TOTAL 227

Fall of Wickets: 1–16, 2–69, 3–89, 4–157, 5–173, 6–187, 7–197, 8–217, 9–226, 10–227.

Bowling: Imran, 23–4–55–2; Sarfraz, 23–4–56–3; Tahir, 12–4–25–1; Qadir, 24–9–39–4; Mudassar, 4–1–6–0.

ENGLAND: Second Innings

D. W. Randall, b Mudassar 9
C. J. Tavaré, c Miandad, b Imran 82
A. J. Lamb, lbw, b Mudassar 0
D. I. Gower, c Wasim Bari, b Mudassar 0
I. T. Botham, c Sarfraz, b Mudassar 69
M. W. Gatting, c Wasim Bari, b Mudassar . . 7
D. R. Pringle, c Miandad, b Qadir 14
I. A. Greig, lbw, b Mudassar 2
E. E. Hemmings, c Wasim Bari, b Imran 14
R. W. Taylor, not out 24
R. D. Jackman, c Haroon, b Qadir 17
Extras (b 10, lb 19, w 5, nb 4) 38

TOTAL 276

Fall of Wickets: 1–9, 2–9, 3–9, 4–121, 5–132, 6–171, 7–180, 8–224, 9–235, 10–276.

Bowling: Imran, 42–13–84–2; Sarfraz, 14–5–22–0; Qadir, 37.5–15–94–2; Mudassar, 19–7–32–6; Tahir, 7–4–6–0.

PAKISTAN: Second Innings

Mohsin Khan, not out 39
Javed Miandad, not out 26
Extras (b 1, lb 10, w 1) 12

TOTAL (no wkt) 77

Bowling: Botham, 7–0–30–0; Jackman, 4–0–20–0; Hemmings, 2.1–0–13–0.

Umpires: H. D. Bird and D. J. Constant.

Pakistan won by 10 wkts.

On such a wicket and with such bowling it was no picnic for Gower, captaining England for the first time. Botham knows the feeling.

Mohsin batted just over eight hours to score the first Test double-hundred at Lord's since Donnelly's for New Zealand in 1949. With Zaheer he put on 153 for the fourth wicket, equalling the Pakistan record against England. At lunch, on the first day, Mohsin was 64 and at close of play 159. He was missed off Botham at slip when 72 but otherwise drove, cut and pulled with rare elegance and power.

Lean and tall, Mohsin plays from his full height, swinging the bat and surging towards the bowler with infectious delight. On form and on a fast pitch he makes batting the most lyrical of arts. His method is such, though, as to expose flaws when the ball is not coming on to him.

LEFT On the second day Jackman reached his 37th birthday. In all he bowled 36 overs to take 4 for 110. On looks, with his lack of inches and his titupping run up, no one would take him for an England opening bowler. But, as with racehorses, looks aren't everything. Jackman is honesty personified, always game, always doing just a little, even on the best of pitches, and never giving up. His method of appealing is ridiculous, but that is another matter.

RIGHT Zaheer, so lordly a player off the back foot and generally so greedy for runs, batted well enough here, but Mohsin had stolen his thunder and he never got it back.

BELOW RIGHT Something has got away but who and where? Or is Taylor admiring a pretty girl in the Grand Stand? Tavaré may be facing Mecca but there's no need to do that at Lord's.

LEFT You can bat like that if you want to, but it's more a fielding attitude, even for Randall.

BELOW LEFT It is not often you see Gower in an inelegant posture but the cares of captaincy seem to have weighed him down.

RIGHT Lamb kept his hair on but not his helmet. Imran tore into him, as he did to Gower, and Lamb for a while looked ready for the slaughter. He was hit on the arm here in one of several ferociously fast spells from Imran.

4

No one has described Qadir better than Donald Woods did in *The Times* of 26 August. 'The eyes narrow ominously and the fringe of dark beard hints at brigandage and plunder ... You could imagine that face emerging from the mystic gloom of a Karachi bazaar to whisper dread tidings of deceit in high places and intrigue in the back streets, and the name Abdul is somehow appropriate ...'

It is indeed. Qadir's action is complementary to his appearance, ritualistic, from the raising of the left hand to herald commencement, to the dying flurry, and mesmeric, as if between dream and hypnosis, the bowler himself repeating the pattern of his delivery down the pitch.

x

8

y

12

z

LEFT Botham, sweeping, is given not out, and Qadir, incensed, begins the kind of aggressive mating dance with accompanying cries that small animals produce in intense frustration.

RIGHT Miandad does a dance of another kind, a little disco paddle, safely out of reach.

BELOW Gatting, hemmed in, finds other avenues. So often he promised well, only to lose his wicket to a dreadful stroke.

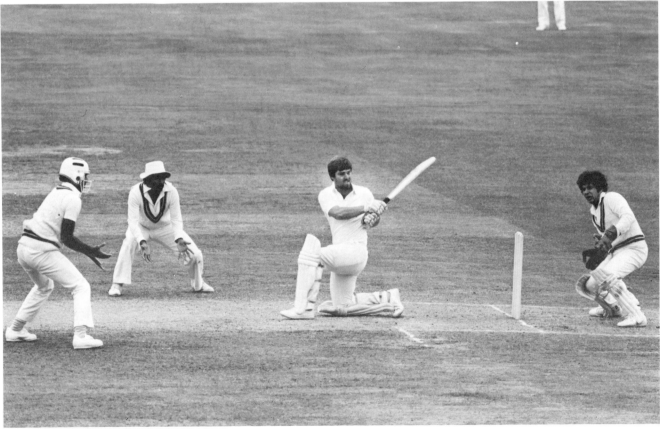

LEFT England have just been bowled out for 227 and will be asked to follow-on. Jackman, out to Imran, seems to have spotted something suspicious in the grass. The umpire, Constant, is worried too. Imran, setting a fine example, began to learn that nothing unites a team so quickly as success. Whatever differences there may have been, the Pakistanis responded increasingly to Imran's romantic leadership.

BELOW Miandad was often in the firing line, though if this unexpected drive from Tavaré went where it looks as if it did he was lucky. Tavaré, in his second innings, batted not much under seven hours for 82. His 50 took 350 minutes, a tortoise-like effort that succeeded in beating his own record for the slowest 50 in a Test in England. Tavaré came near to saving the match for England by his skeletal patience, and if he had played earlier half as fluently as he did in his last 20 minutes, he would certainly have done so. What is odd about Tavaré is that when he opens up he bats quite as safely as when he drops his bat lugubriously on half-volleys hour after hour. There is little wrong with his technique, despite an awkward grip, and when he uses his feet and lets the bat go through, one can see an attractive player struggling to be let out.

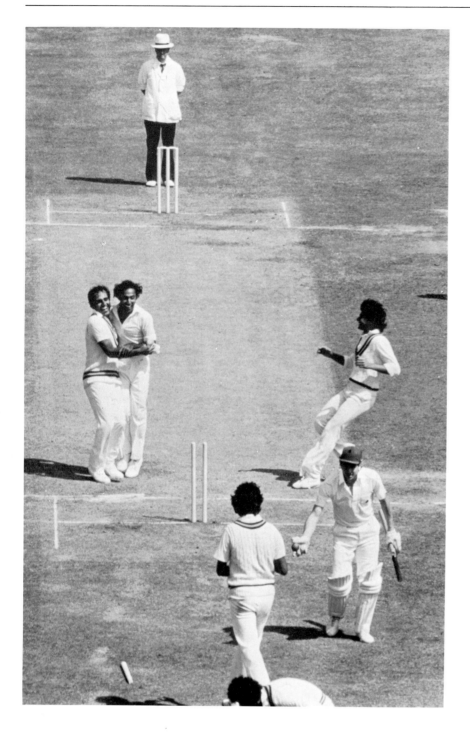

Mudassar, in England's second innings, removed Randall, Lamb and Gower in six balls. In the first of the three pictures, Randall has lost his off stump, courteously picking the ball up; in the second, Lamb is lbw two balls later; and in the third,

Gower is caught at the wicket off a neurotic prod to a ball well wide of him. Mudassar's jump of joy is scarcely surprising. It must have been almost too much like a dream to be true. He rarely bowls, even for Cheshire, and his methods, on so good a pitch, are

not normally of the kind to surprise competent batsmen, let alone class Test cricketers. But Mudassar surprised England more than once; obviously Imran, too, who could rarely bring himself to call on him. Sometimes, for a couple of overs,

he was so innocuous and pointless that he was taken off immediately. But here, as in the second innings at Headingley, he had moments of magic which, even if they don't come again, he can never forget. His approach is enthusiastically amiable,

culminating in a sideways leap which takes him to the extreme edge of the crease. From this point he swivels inward, brushing his ear with his arm, the ball slanting in to the batsman from the line of mid-off. Sometimes it continues

harmlessly on course, occasionally it holds up and ducks in sharply. The odd one hustles off the pitch and goes the other way.

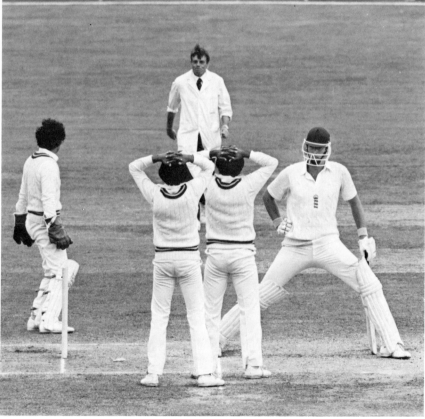

LEFT Not a new dance from the Khyber, but uniformity of response to the turning down of an appeal for stumping. Pringle had no more idea than Greig about how to play Qadir and he was exceptionally fortunate that Imran allowed him an hour's freedom from him. As soon as Qadir came on, Pringle was gone, Miandad virtually picking the ball off the splice as it hit. Pringle's figures against India and Pakistan were scarcely encouraging; a top score of 23 in five innings, and only seven wickets in 108 overs at a cost of 40. But he was picked on promise and on promise he was chosen for Australia.

RIGHT Botham has got away with something pretty sneaky here and he knows it. In fact Qadir has beaten both him and Wasim Bari, not for the first time. Without being quite at his best – no sixes – Botham still managed to score 100 runs in the match.

ABOVE Mohsin receiving his award as Man of the Match. There was really no other candidate, though no one contributed more by personal effort than did Imran, or by psychological pressure than Qadir. But what about Mudassar? Six for 32 as third change bowler – can that really be right?

RIGHT Pakistanis have a lot to put up with in England. If at times their support seemed childishly shrill, it was good to see them so deservedly happy.

ENGLAND vs PAKISTAN

THIRD TEST

HEADINGLEY (26–31 August)

This crucial match, as well as being the decider between two evenly matched teams, was England's last chance to solve outstanding problems before the party for Australia was chosen. Willis was fit to return as captain, and Marks and Fowler came in for Pringle, Greig and Hemmings. Pringle was unfit, Greig had a wretched match at Lord's, and Hemmings failed to take a wicket. The choice of Fowler, the 25-year-old Lancashire opening batsman who only got his county cap in 1981, allowed Randall to drop down the order, which after Lords was inevitable if he were to be kept at all.

For Pakistan Majid Khan, Sikander Bakht and the portly 32-year-old Ehtesham-ud-Din, recruited from the Lancashire league in the continued absence of Sarfraz, replaced Haroon Rashid, Tahir Naqqash and Sarfraz.

As in 1981 the Headingley Test was a game of extraordinary fluctuations and relentless tension. England won it, but there were moments on the fourth and fifth days when Pakistan came near to doing to England what England did to Australia in not dissimilar circumstances.

Fowler, in the event, was a success. Otherwise only Gower and Botham, in their first innings, batted with much distinction for England. For Pakistan, Javed Miandad and Imran Khan each played two good innings, and Mudassar one.

In general, it was a bowler's match, the ball usually swinging under variable cloud. The spinners scarcely had a look in, Marks bowling only 7 overs in the match, and Qadir, though he bowled 30 overs altogether, taking only 1 for 103 for his pains. Jackman, Botham and Willis did nearly all the bowling for England and though Jackman only took 4 wickets to Willis's 6 and Botham's 9 he bowled the longest and the most accurately when it really mattered.

PAKISTAN: First Innings

Mohsin Khan, c Taylor, b Botham	10
Mudassar Nazar, b Botham	65
Mansoor Akhtar, c Gatting, b Willis	0
Javed Miandad, c Fowler, b Willis	54
Zaheer Abbas, c Taylor, b Jackman	8
Majid Khan, lbw, b Jackman	21
Imran Khan, not out	67
Wasim Bari, b Jackman	23
Abdul Qadir, c Willis, b Botham	5
Sikander Bakht, c Tavaré, b Willis	7
Ehtesham-ud-Din, b Botham	0
Extras (b 1, lb 7, w 4, nb 3)	15

TOTAL 275

Fall of Wickets: 1–16, 2–19, 3–119, 4–128, 5–160, 6–168, 7–207, 8–224, 9–274, 10–275.

Bowling: Willis, 26–6–76–3; Botham, 24.5–9–70–4; Jackman, 37–14–74–3; Marks, 5–0–23–0; Gatting, 8–2–17–0.

ENGLAND: First Innings

C. J. Tavaré, c sub, b Imran	22
G. Fowler, b Ehtesham	9
M. W. Gatting, lbw, b Imran	25
A. J. Lamb, c Mohsin, b Imran	0
D. I. Gower, c sub, b Sikander	74
I. T. Botham, c sub, b Sikander	57
D. W. Randall, run out	8
V. J. Marks, b Qadir	7
R. W. Taylor, c Miandad, b Imran	18
R. D. Jackman, c Mohsin, b Imran	11
R. G. D. Willis, not out	1
Extras (b 4, lb 10, w 2, nb 8)	24

TOTAL 256

Fall of Wickets: 1–15, 2–67, 3–69, 4–77, 5–146, 6–159, 7–170, 8–209, 9–255, 10–256.

Bowling: Imran, 25.2–7–49–5; Ehtesham, 14–4–46–1; Sikander, 24–5–47–2; Qadir, 22–5–87–1; Mudassar, 4–1–3–0.

PAKISTAN: Second Innings

Mohsin Khan, c Taylor, b Willis	0
Mudassar Nazar, c Botham, b Willis	0
Mansoor Akhtar, c Randall, b Botham	39
Javed Miandad, c Taylor, b Botham	52
Zaheer Abbas, lbw, b Botham	4
Majid Khan, c Gower, b Botham	10
Imran Khan, c Randall, b Botham	46
Wasim Bari, c Taylor, b Willis	7
Abdul Qadir, b Jackman	17
Sikander Bakht, c Gatting, b Marks	7
Ehtesham-ud-Din, not out	0
Extras (lb 6, w 4, nb 7)	17

TOTAL 199

Fall of Wickets: 1–0, 2–3, 3–81, 4–85, 5–108, 6–115, 7–128, 8–169, 9–199, 10–199.

Bowling: Willis, 19–3–55–3; Botham, 30–8–74–5; Jackman, 28–11–41–1; Gatting, 2–1–4–0; Marks, 2–1–8–1.

ENGLAND: Second Innings

C. J. Tavaré, c Majid, b Imran	33
G. Fowler, c Wasim Bari, b Mudassar	86
M. W. Gatting, lbw, b Imran	25
A. J. Lamb, b Mudassar	4
D. I. Gower, c Wasim Bari, b Mudassar	7
I. T. Botham, c Majid, b Mudassar	4
D. W. Randall, lbw, b Imran	0
V. J. Marks, not out	12
R. W. Taylor, not out	6
Extras (b 19, lb 16, w 1, nb 6)	42

TOTAL (7 wkts) 219

R. D. Jackman and R. G. D. Willis did not bat.

Fall of Wickets: 1–103, 2–168, 3–172, 4–187, 5–189, 6–198, 7–199.

Bowling: Sikander, 20–4–40–0; Imran, 30.2–8–66–3; Qadir, 8–2–16–0; Mudassar, 22–7–55–4.

Umpires: D. J. Constant and B. J. Meyer.

England won by 3 wkts.

Fowler, having dived forward at cover to grasp a mis-cue from Miandad, gets his name in a Test scoresheet for the first time. Although he lasted only 25 minutes in his first innings Fowler's 86 in the second – taking hm 2 hours 21 minutes – set England comfortably along the path to victory. It was scarcely to be expected that 5 wickets would subsequently fall for 21 runs. Fowler was born in Accrington, went to the Grammar School there, and thence to Durham University.

LEFT Miandad played one of his more responsible innings, batting nearly four hours for 54. Jackman could not quite hang on to this one, one of the rare occasions when Miandad trusted the swing enough to drive.

RIGHT Jackman adds the wicket of Wasim Bari to those of Zaheer and Majid. Altogether he bowled 37 overs in the innings. This gesture was both unnecessary and discourteous, as he must instantly have recognised.

BELOW Willis, unlike Fletcher, in similar circumstances but with different players in India, was quick to take Jackman to task. Willis surprised everyone agreeably by his easy yet authoritative way of captaining and his comparative attention to detail. His own form, with bat and ball, showed no decline.

LEFT Miandad's first fifty was a prolonged battle of wits, his second, taking only a third of the time, a dazzling display of hitting off the back foot and square cutting. Botham came in for plenty of stick and altogether Miandad hit nine 4s off only 57 balls.

BELOW LEFT Fowler's pleasure at catching him was obviously shared by Randall, Lamb, Tavaré and Willis.

RIGHT Botham, when not under fire from Miandad, was never easy to play. He moved the ball both ways off a length and beat the batsman outside the off stump times without number.

BELOW RIGHT Imran having just hooked Jackman for six, Willis called up Botham to polish off the innings. This he did by bowling Ehtesham-ud-Din off his helmet. There is little sentimentality or compassion in Botham's cricketing make-up.

Gatting makes Miandad hop. His two innings of 25 were not enough, however, to earn him a trip to Australia. No one had more persuasive advocates in the Press than Gatting, who did everything required of him except make a big score. In 6 innings his highest score was 32 not out, yet on most occasions he looked to be batting sensibly and well. Gatting scored massively for Middlesex, took a number of wickets with his medium-paced bowling, and held plenty of catches. There seems no reason to doubt his temperament, so his continued semi-failure at Test level remains something of a puzzle.

ABOVE There are several leapers among the Pakistan bowlers but Sikander really does seem to take off.

RIGHT Fowler, after a promising start, had his off stump hit by Ehtesham-ud-Din. This was Ehtesham's solitary moment of glory. He had already been clunked on the head by Botham and was soon to pull a muscle after Botham had savagely hooked him several times in a row. On his next appearance – escorted by a runner – Ehtesham looked more suited to a spell at Baden-Baden than a walk to the wicket.

Randall has called for a single but been sent back by Fowler. Sikander races in and throws the wicket down. Randall was out second ball to Imran for 0 in his last innings of the series.

BELOW Imran, having done most of the bowling, must have expected that, at least occasionally his batting might have been a pleasurable bonus. But time after time he found himself obliged to put as much into his batting as he had done into his bowling. He rarely failed to show by example. He is a correct, thoughtful batsman, able, when necessary, to hit sixes over the bowler's head with delightful ease. He is a compulsive hooker and often falls in county cricket to a sucker long-hop. He usually wears a pale blue or white helmet; a pity, for like many of his team-mates, he is good to look upon. Since 1978 he has done wonders for Sussex. He was born in Lahore in 1952, is a cousin of Majid, and captained Oxford. Undemonstrative on the field, he moves and performs with the lithe elegance of the natural athlete.

RIGHT Whatever portion of Botham's anatomy umpire Meyer is examining, it is plainly causing concern. Willis commiserates. It can happen to all of us.

LEFT Sikander gets airborne when batting as well as bowling. Willis, and Botham, too, when he feels like it, can make the best of them hop. The bat is resolutely, and protectively, straight.

RIGHT Sikander is given out, caught by Gatting at short leg off Marks. Sikander had resisted bravely to help Imran add 30 and bring Pakistan right back into the reckoning. If endless television replays are anything to go by, this was the worst, and from Pakistan's point of view the most damaging and inexcusable decision of the series.

BELOW RIGHT Runs for Imran, a restorative press-up for Willis, and a gentle stroll for the umpire.

Fowler looked a neat, compact player off his legs and a fluent striker of the ball to the off. Qadir seems to have got one past him (*right*) judging by Wasim Bari's expression, or it may be just relief at having saved another four byes. Imran, Mudassar, Sarfraz and Qadir all had Wasim jumping about like a jack-in-a-box, the faster bowlers spraying the ball with some speed and swing, and Qadir sending him sprawling in all directions with his deceptive spin.

Imran has just removed Gatting lbw for the second time in the match. Ten of the Pakistan players are visible in this picture, a more seemly expression of satisfaction than some that could have been printed. It is commonplace for footballers to have their hair permed, and to jump on one another after a goal is scored like copulating monkeys, but cricketers could go in the same direction if they're not careful. Too gloating a pleasure in dismissals, bullying appeals, ill-manners towards opponents, dissent over decisions, are among the things that cricket can well do without. Imran, who had such a marvellous summer, made a tactical mistake in complaining about the umpiring, no matter how justified the circumstance. English umpires are fallible, but Imran has travelled enough to know what kind of local pressure umpires suffer in India, Pakistan, Australia and the West Indies, and the effect it has on them.

One of Botham's more amiable gestures. His grins vary from the wolfish to the surly, but on occasion glimpses of pure pleasure and simple good nature lighten the ferocity. He was not, against Pakistan, quite the force he was against Australia and India, but he did well enough. Imran decisively upstaged him, which was probably no bad thing for once.

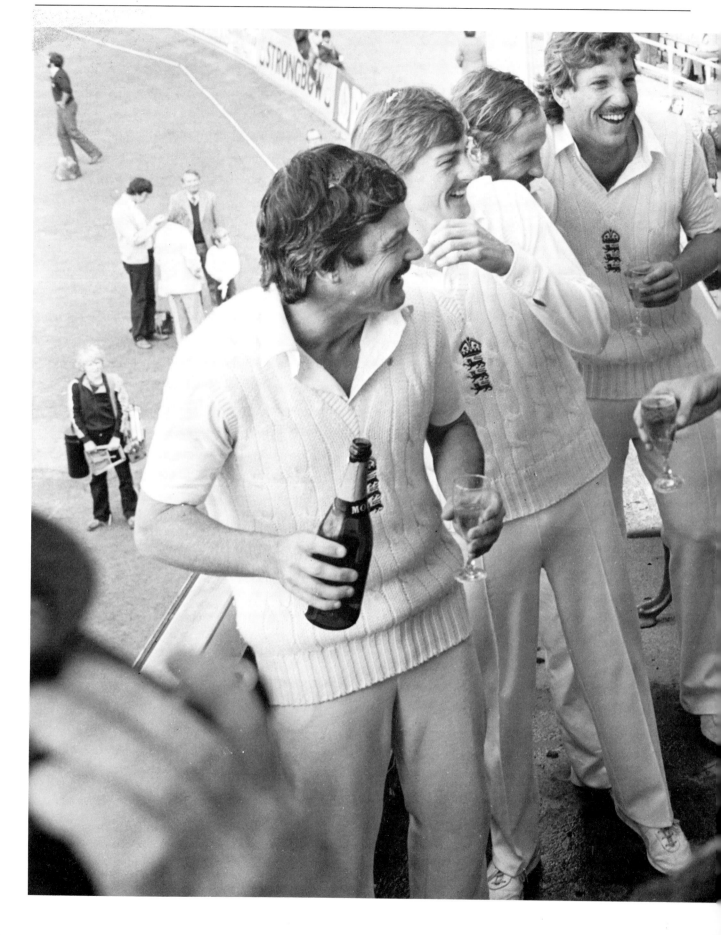

The end of a hard-fought series, a double summer of Test matches, county matches, one-day leagues, and cut-throat competitions. Willis came out of it satisfactorily and so, more or less, did England. Two great international stars emerged in Kapil Dev and Imran Khan, and both India and Pakistan made many friends. A drink is certainly called for and Willis, for one, will be glad to put his feet up before he puts them down again on the hard grounds of Australia.

EXTRAS

Test Matches are not the only thing. Middlesex, in Brearley's last season, won the Championship. At half-way Middlesex looked too far ahead to be caught, certainly by Leicestershire whom they led by 61 points. But Leicestershire, coming with a late rush, took it to the final match. Somerset won the Benson and Hedges and, both finals equally one-sided, Surrey the Natwest Trophy. Sussex, one-day champions in early Gillette days, won the John Player league for the first time, with a record number of points. Cambridge beat Oxford after three declarations.

When everything that could have been decided had been, the Oldtimers came to the Oval. An Indian summer descended just too late to warm their bones and gild their white hairs. Still, they enjoyed themselves and wound back the years for those who watched them.

Every September marks the end for somebody, every May the start for someone else. These pictures record some milestones: retirements, birthday parties, comebacks. Fittingly, in this great summer of all-rounders, two of the greatest engaged in friendly combat. There was nothing Sobers could not do, except perhaps a reverse sweep. Botham has yet to bowl a Chinaman.

Cricket isn't usually quite such a mess, but in one-day stuff anything can happen. Gower is at the bottom of this heap, and Kirmani and Yashpal Sharmar contributing to it. You could say that by the end Kirmani is sitting pretty, though that boot in the ribs can't be comfortable. Perhaps he's levitating. The occasion was the Prudential Trophy match between England and India at the Oval. England won all four of the one-day internationals.

BELOW It's lucky these two aren't traffic cops. As it is, the poor devil responsible for shifting sightscreens at Edgbaston scarcely knows whether he's coming or going. The semaphore signallers are David Bairstow and David Smith, the occasion the Natwest semi-final between Warwickshire and Yorkshire. Despite Bairstow's efforts Smith made a hundred.

RIGHT The scoreboard certainly bears a crook look. Asif Din and Gladstone Small are running for all their worth, but though they put on 62 together Warwickshire could not make a match of the Natwest final.

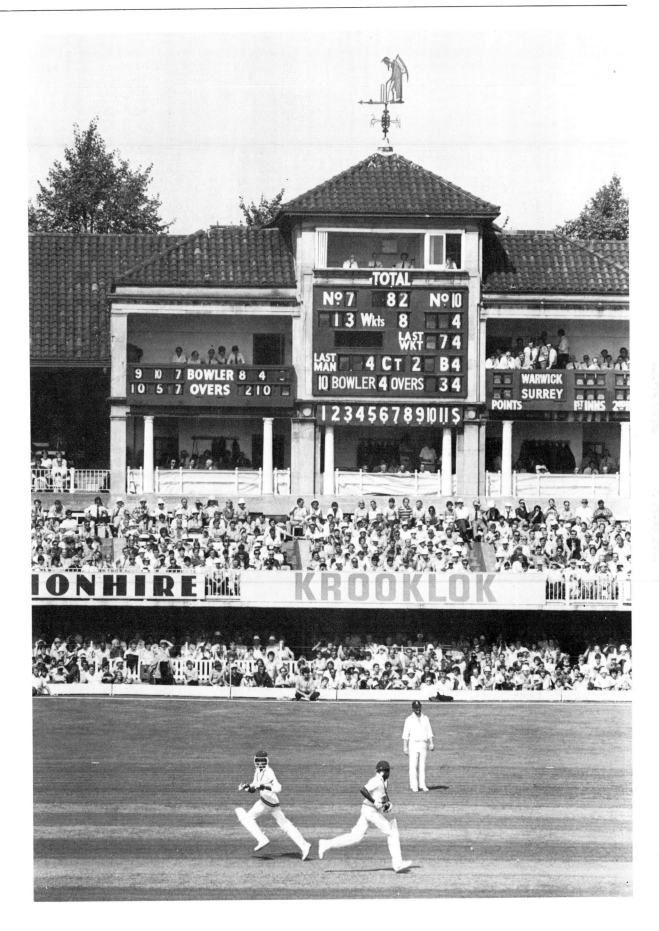

ABOVE Ray Illingworth, at the age of 50, returns to the field, demonstrating that a man on the spot is worth ten in the pavilion. Under him, Yorkshire prospered.

RIGHT Middlesex have tied up the Championship and Brearley, a mere 40-year-old, has added the final laurel to his crown. The pioneer of the helmet doffs it for the last time. Runs flowed in his farewell season as smoothly from Brearley's bat as the swans on the river past Worcester Cathedral.

Some were stouter, some greyer, some balder, but their names made sweet music. Anyone who has ever watched Sobers and Kanhai bat could recognise them even if their faces had been masked out. They never wore helmets. They were as free as air. Their strokes were indelible.

RIGHT Barbados vs The Rest, The Oval, 18 September.
Back row: Greenidge, Haynes, Marshall, King, Garner, Clarke, Padmore, Hope.
Front row: Holder, Hall, Sobers, Griffiths, Nurse.

BELOW RIGHT Old England vs Old Rest of the World, The Oval, 19 September.
Back row: Graveney, Snow, Lindwall, Kanhai, Marshall, Griffiths, Harvey, Pataudi, Close, Clark, Sobers, Engineer, D'Oliveira, Hall, Edrich, Gibbs, Murray.
Front row: Trueman, Parfitt, Wilson, Simpson, Denness, Sharpe.

On 31 July, G. O. Allen, who played 25 times for England, eleven times as captain, was 80. On 9 August, M.C.C. gave a dinner at Lord's for this great all-rounder of the 1930s, who for seven years after the war was Chairman of the Test selectors and for 14 years Treasurer of M.C.C. He has also been President. The last such dinner was given for Plum Warner's 80th in 1953, when C. B. Fry proposed the toast. This time it was Lord Home, who was in the Eton XI of 1921 with Allen. Not often is such an array of talent seen even on the sacred turf of Lord's, especially in black ties. The scoreboard tells the story.

Back row: M. J. K. Smith, Ted Dexter, Tom Graveney, Alec Bedser, Freddie Brown, Basil D'Oliveira.

Front row: George Mann, Godfrey Evans, Denis Compton, Len Hutton, Gubby Allen, Leslie Ames, Peter May, Jim Laker.

Indoors candles, presidents,
prime ministers, and tales of long
ago.

RIGHT In their heyday,
formidable rivals: Denis
Compton, Sir Leonard Hutton,
Keith Miller, Bill Edrich.

The Agatha Christie Trophy. Tests between Young West Indian and Young English (under 19) cricketers have been going on since 1974. West Indies won this series 2–0. England stars of the future – joining such as Gooch, Gatting, Gower, Miller and Tavaré from earlier encounters – look like being Illingworth, a left-arm spin bowler from Worcestershire, Folley, a quick bowler from Lancashire, Capel, an all-rounder from Northamptonshire, and the captain Potter, already a consistent runmaker for Kent. The West Indians, coached by Seymour Nurse, contained an assortment of leg-spinners and googly merchants, off-spinners and classic, left-arm bowlers, to say nothing of two formidable fast bowlers, Ferris and Walsh. Sadly, helmets are already in use by close fielders and the England players, emulating their elders, more than once dissented volubly from umpiring decisions.

Norman Cowans. Well might he look thoughtful. Jamaican-born, but at the age of 21 in the England party for Australia. Six-foot three, and in his first full season for Middlesex Cowans represents the new generation. Impressively quick on occasion, he still looks next to Daniel – five years his senior – something of a beanpole. When he fills out, who knows but that he may not provide England with a first taste of their own real West Indian pace.